The Prophetic Anointing

The Prophetic
Anointing

Perry L. Harrington

Copyright © 2009 by Perry L. Harrington.

ISBN: Softcover   978-1-4415-8369-7

All rights reserved. No part of this book may be reproduced or transmitted in any form or by any means, electronic or mechanical, including photocopying, recording, or by any information storage and retrieval system, without permission in writing from the copyright owner.

This book was printed in the United States of America.

To order additional copies of this book, contact:
Xlibris Corporation
1-888-795-4274
www.Xlibris.com
Orders@Xlibris.com
68188

Dedication and Acknowledgements:

I dedicate this book to the one who endowed me with the gift and the ability to interpret and write. Jesus Christ the author and finisher of my faith. Thank You for entrusting me with such a great gift. I am forever thankful!

I dedicate this, my first book to my wife of 29 years, Felecia. For all your love and support, You have been a strong pillar of encouragement and inspiration and I am truly grateful.

To all the men and women of God that deposited into my life and contributed in countless ways to my experiences in writing this book: the late Elder Marion D. Dantzler, Bishop Allen H. Simmons, Bishop Jerry T. Hardison, Prophetess Frances D. Hardison, Apostle David A.A. Mungo, Pastor Robert A. Jones, Pastor Jean Sellers, Teacher Ernest Jackson, Bishop Alfred E. Williams, to all those that helped push me to my destined place, and to all others too numerous to name, Thank you! And to my mother, Mother Caroline Harrington, thanks mom!

In Memory of:

Elder Marion D. Dantzler
Deacon John Peay, Jr
Missionary Marian J. Peay
Apostle King Sellers, Jr.
Dr. Thomas Dawkins

These writings are inspired by Holy Scriptures, personal experiences and teachings from renowned and proven prophets of God. All scriptures are taken from the original King James Version of the Holy Bible. For many years there has been a extremely large amount of controversy about the prophetic move of God, in the earth. After reading this book you should have a great deal of clarity and understanding concerning the operations of the prophet, which we will also call the prophetic anointing.

Let's begin with some simple definitions: first, the prophet is defined as a messenger of God, who is able to *foretell* or *forthtell,* A predictor of future events but not limited to that ability only, The prophet operates on a spontaneous unction of the Holy Spirit which enables him or her to speak the things of God at almost any given time. We will get greater depths as we go further.

The prophetic is ended with the suffix—ic, which means of, pertaining to, or characterized by. So we conclude to say prophetic is of the prophet and characterized by the prophet. Let's briefly consider the *Anointing*. The *Anointing* is taken from the root word anoint. Which means to smear, pour, or cover with oil. This symbolizes consecration and appointment to a certain office. The anointing is empowerment to operate in a particular office or vocation. By experience I have seen people operate in the prophetic but have never professed to be a prophet. This allows us to know that God uses whom He will at any given time. If we are willing vessels, God will operate as He finds it necessary. By yielding ourselves to God, while operating in ministry, God will reveal things to us and give us insight on many aspects of life. This is what many call revelation knowledge.

My first encounter of the prophetic was when I was around 20 years old. I was at a church on a Friday evening. I hadn't even confessed Christ as my Lord and Savior. The pastor called me to the front and stretched out his hand and said, "preach my revelation". I remember grabbing both sides of my head and going slowing down to the floor. This was the first time I had ever been in a Pentecostal church. I had never seen any pentecostals in operation, so I know I wasn't imitating what I had seen somewhere else like many do today. In fact this encounter happen after a church play given by the youth department. This is defined as *"forthtelling"*. I was being called forth. Ministry was being called forth in me and it was done by the unction of the Holy Spirit. From that moment my life was revolutionized. I was blessed with an instant hunger and thirst for righteousness and deeply compelled to preach God's word. I received Christ as my Savior about 2 weeks later and began a new life in Christ. My heart was convicted by the power of the prophetic anointing.

Ephesians 4:11 describes the fivefold ministry gifts: *"And He gave some Apostles, and some Prophets, and some Evangelists, and some Pastors and Teachers"*. No one should ever think that one is greater than the other. All ministry gifts are to compliment the other, working together to make the hand of God. In the natural, if any finger is missing from the hand we would miss it. We would not realize it's importance until it is gone, because each finger plays a vital role in the hand. If then the ministry gifts are listed in chronological order, then the prophet would be in the position of the index finger, second in order. Keep in mind that the five ministry gifts help makes the hand of God. In the music field as well as the medical, the fingers of the hand are numbered beginning with the thumb, being one. The index finger is two, middle finger is three, the ring finger is four and the little or pinky finger is five. According to a scripture Ephesians 4:11, the Prophet is second, which concludes that it's the index finger. With the index finger we use it to point. It is our forefinger and it is the most sensitive. Therefore the character of the prophetic incorporates foretelling, also the Prophet should be considered most sensitive that the prophet points out things, circumstances, conditions, problems, the will of God and so forth. God endows every believer as He will with various gifts, talents and abilities. They are designed to sustain us while we, the believers are here on the earth.

As we refer back to Ephesians chapter 4 in verse 12, we see that the purpose is also to make the believer "perfect". Now we have heard the quotation "nobody is perfect", what we should say instead is that "nobody is flawless". It is God's will for every believer to be perfect. The word perfect here is referring to being complete and mature. It doesn't mean that we won't make mistakes and bad choices, or miss God's timing. But absolute obedience to the word of God will eventually makes us mature and complete. The gifts are our tools and weapons of work and warfare. The gifts are given for the edifying of the body. To edify means to build up and to strengthen with encouragement. For how long? Verse 13 states that until we all come into the unity of the faith and the knowledge of the Son of God. Also it states that until we come unto a perfect man and that our stature measures the same stature of Christ. Sadly to say that today some believers are seeking the usage of these gifts to bring comfort and gratification mainly for their personal lives.

The Prophetic Anointing enables a believer to operate prophetically, which means one can operate as a Prophet but not neccessarily be a Prophet. Because of the urgency of the times, God is doing a quick work and sending soul piercing messages in the world in order to reap an end time harvest of souls. So therefore the prophetic must take the center stage and proclaim the infallible word of God.

As a believer I encountered the second experience shortly after I received Christ as my Savior. I was serving as a musician at the church I was attending. As the Pastor spoke a word concerning my music (*foretell*), at that time there was not a lot of upbeat gospel like it is today. The Pastor spoke about the future state of my music and how it would be a part of the "new" music that was approaching the house of God and the gospel music field. And today many musicians are using the techniques that God blessed me with many years ago. The prophetic is classified among the vocal gifts. It is the power of the spoken word (*RHEMA*) under the unction the Holy Spirit.

The word of God is given in two major forms even though God cannot be limited in His abilities. Let's consider the two forms of God's word: the Greek word *'logos'* which means the written word and *'rhema'* which means the spoken word. There are many examples of God's spoken word in action when we search the Holy Scriptures.

Let's take out this time to look into Ezekiel 37. The Prophet Ezekiel was taken by the hand of God into the valley of dry bones. After Ezakiel's confidence and dependence upon God was confirmed in verse 3, God told him to prophesy to the bones. Ezekiel spoke life and restoration upon the bones *(foretell)*. After which Ezekiel was commanded to prophesy to the winds *(forthtell)* and the bones stood up as a mighty army. In this passage of scripture we see the prophetic in action in foretelling and in forthtelling. Ezekiel told the bones about their future state, then Ezekiel calls forth the wind to breathe life into the bones. Another area in the prophetic is the area of confirmation. When a person is dealing with something on the inside, it could be something that they are worried about or something they are contemplating or needing to make a decision about. It could be something that maybe tormenting them on the inside. Whatever the case may be, a word of confirmation brings the things from the inside out to the forefront, in other words, inward things are revealed.

When I was called by God to preach His word, I was exposed to my third encounter of the prophetic anointing. I was carrying this burden on the inside, and this burden was getting heavy. When God was calling me, I didn't know how or when to come forth. Our ministry had relocated to another town but we had the same pastor. One Saturday morning the men of the church were having prayer, I was in the number. After the prayer the pastor stood up and said that, "Soon Brother Harrington will have an announcement for the whole church". That was when I knew, the calling of God was confirmed through the pastor. About 2 weeks later I preached my introductory sermon.

Jesus walked in the prophetic in every aspect, while the major and minor prophets of the scripture were limited in abilities. One instant when Jesus operated in the word of confirmation, was in John 4:16-19 as He confirmed to the Samaritan at Jacob's well about her marital situation. As He did so she stated that she perceived Him as a Prophet. That was something the woman had been dealing with on the inside and was revealed so that God would get the glory. The prophetic today is the same as it was in the "days of old". Jesus was and is the only biblical Prophet that was unlimited in His abilities. One should beware of anyone claiming to "see all and know all". The prophetic anointing is not designed to make us commercial misfits or to offer gimmicks. God uses the Prophet as He wills so that is why we will discover that no matter how intense the anointing may be, we are still subject to the Highest power. The spirit of the prophet is subject to prophet. There are times when God will reveal a thing to the prophet and the prophet is instructed not to say anything about what he or she has seen or heard about a particular person or thing. There are times when revelation is given to the prophet to keep the prophet in safety and to enlighten him or her on who or what they are dealing with, especially when the prophet is operating in the ministry of preaching. God has often used the prophet as one that brings a word of warning. Usually in the today's church, a word of warning is not appreciated to the fullest. Most people expect the prophet to speak a word of promise usually with prosperity being involved in the promise. Promises of houses, cars, land and money. They are looking for things that will bring comfort to their lives. We also have to realize that if we believe the prophet we shall prosper so even if the prophet brings warning to God's people, we should not be offended and discouraged. We should be encouraged to take the word of God in, the word will be a lamp unto our feet and a light unto our pathway. (Psalms 119:105).

The second finger on the hand points out, so does it with the hand of God. The prophet points out and points to. What does this mean? Well, the prophets word sometimes points us into the direction in which the Lord desires or commands us to go. So when the prophet is preaching, teaching or prophesying their operation should be that of pointing out or pointing to.

Many have asked the questions: What causes the prophetic anointing to become active? How is it stirred up? What releases it to to flow? There are three sure ways to get the prophetic anointing to begin to move.

First let's look at the 3 P's: prayer, praise and preaching. First, prayer brings us in communion with God. We are communicating to God when we pray remember powerful prayer is a two way conversation. We communicate with God and God communicates with us. A monologue conversation means that only one person is talking. A dialogue is when two people talk to each other. One talk as the other listens, then the opportunity comes when the listener gets a chance to talk. When we pray we should not only just talk and make requests to God, but we should also listen to what God has to say. Note that God speaks to us for various reasons other than just prophesying. If we are seeking God to move in the prophetic, as we pray we give an attentive ear that we may hear what the Spirit of God is saying. As the prophet or believer hears God, the Holy Spirit that dwells within them begins to act as an editor and monitor, revealing to the hearer what should or should not be spoken.

Referring back to the hand of God and the prophet being the second finger, the index finger, that is the most sensitive finger on the hand. The prophet is the most sensitive of the fivefold ministry gifts. The sensitivity of the prophet allows him or her to be in touch with the voice of God with precise clarity and accuracy. Those of us who believe the prophets and believe in the prophetic move of God, should be able to trust those that minister in this manner.

When the prophet prays, it's not always the purpose of the prophet to hear a word from the Lord. Sometimes the word may be given to the prophet without them expecting a word to come. This is what is called a 'spontaneous' word. Sometimes the prophet can pray seeking an answer about a particular thing. An answer may or may not come but if it does, this is called a 'sought after word'. We respond differently to the spontaneous and the sought after word. The spontaneous word gives God all the glory. It appears that there is no room for error when God moves spontaneously. A sought after word could tempt the prophet to take credit for something that God has done. We will discuss this in detail as we go further.

In order to get a clear understanding about this, let's look at the definition of spontaneous. It is simply defined as: arising from a momentary impulse. It is also defined as: produced without human labor. From these definitions taken from the Merrian-Webster Collegiate Dictionary, we conclude that the spontaneous move of God is moving as He wills. It is not about control thus thinking that God is a genie in a lamp. God gives us what we need at the time when we need it, even if it seems like it is too late. God is still on time! Those who seek God for answers, especially when seeking God for others, can easily be tempted to think that something was done on their part that activated God for answers. We should never attempt to take any credit for what God has done or for what He is doing in our behalf. Remember that the true workings of the prophetic brings glory to God. The false workings of the prophetic brings attention to the one who is suppose to be operating in that anointing. People will sometimes give a person undeserved acknowledgment for their labor in the ministry. One that is wise will give the glory back to God immediately, for instance, let's say a servant of God has been used mightily by God in the prophetic during a church service. A person could walk up to him or her and give all sorts of compliments. The servant at that moment has the option either to take in those compliments and use them as ego boosters or just tell the individual, "to God be the glory" or just say, pray for me. This will instantly reverse all the glory back to God. It is His work and He should get all the glory for it.

Let's consider another way that the prophetic anointing is set into motion: the area and ministry of praise. The bible says that God inhabits the praise of His people, Israel. (Psalms 22:3). It is a place where God dwells. The praises that go up before God varies in levels and they differ from one believer to another. There are many ways that men praise God. The most important factor in our praise is our sincerity. When we acknowledge God for what He has done, we are coming before His presence with thanksgiving. When we begin to express our love toward God we are now entering into His courts with praise. When we enter into God's courts we begin to enter into his divine presence. When we do this, it clears the line for us to communicate with God. We must keep in mind that God always wants to keep in touch with us. I myself can recall on many occasions when the prophetic anointing fell upon people while the praises of God was being offered. Many orthodox sects of Christian worship begs to differ in the activity of raising the praises of God to such a level. They rule it as unruly, out of order, some feel that it is even disgusting. Some believe that praising God at such a level is merely an emotional high and only brings a person to experience vain imaginations and false manifestations of divine power. However, I have seen and experienced first hand God's divine power in the prophetic during times when praises were offered up to Him. God is a Spirit, and they that worship Him must worship Him in spirit and truth. (John 4:24). Praising God is a part of worship. It is the part that allows us to acknowledge God for His mighty acts. When we praise God in the spirit, divine spiritual energy is released in our surroundings and an atmosphere is created. When an atmosphere is created

God's divine manifestsions occur. Praises offered to God really does cause His Divine power to manifest and not only in the prophetic. God's divine power manifests in all of the ministry gifts, when true praises are offered up to Him.

In the new millenium various forms of praises in the dance have come to the forefront. Various dance teams and dance ministries have surfaced and they cover ever aspect of culture. One in particular is the prophetic dance. When I first witnessed this type of dance I didn't see any difference between the prophetic dance and any other liturgical dance. The dancers moved to the words of the song expressing what the words were saying just like any other liturgical dance, but then I realized these dancers were not just dancing, but they were ministering a message. A message and not just any message but a prophetic message. A message of hope and consolation and also confirmation. When these type of dances are presented to an audience or congregation there is someone in that group who will be blessed by the message being delivered through the dance and lyrics of the song.

I have witnessed the prophetic manifest when the praises of God were offered up with musical instruments. When this was done the man of God declared that God had spoken through the music, I have never tried to limit the benefits of anointed music,but it seemed unbelievable at the time. Understand,ther is a very thin line between inspiration and revelation. As a church musician for over 20 years, I have witnessed anointed music inspire people to a place where they really make definite connections to God in the spirit. This connection causes spiritual eyes and ears to open and that's when revelation takes place, of course music does not effect everyone the same way and neither does God effect everyone the same way. The bible states, "according to your faith be it unto you".(Matthew 9:29). Man should not attempt to put God in a box and think or believe that He moves only a certain way all the time. There are persons that minister in the prophetic through music and since the prophetic is a vocal gift then it it safe to say that singing or speaking repetitiously would get a prophetic message across. The prophetic anointing sometimes causes the psalmist or musician to detour from practice or rehearsal. The prophetic psalmist or musician possess an extraordinary ability to sing and play at a moments notice and without any formal training. By using divine intervention the prophetic psalmist or musician is able to go deep into the spirit of a person even the very soul. They are able to produce encouragement, relief, hope, inspiration, peace, deliverance, shackles can be broken, and things that bind people up can actually be loosed when anointed singing and music is rendered. When the prophetic is in action before and after the word of God has been preached or taught, anointed music can be played to assist in setting and maintaining the kind of atmosphere for a move of God.

When we speak of the prophetic we are foretelling or forthtelling. Usually we think that the prophetic can only be experienced in a church service. This is when the move and workings of God are mostly received, because of the intense atmosphere that is produced when multiple gifts are in operation we tend to think that God will only move during a church environment or maybe a revival or tent crusade. When the word of God is preached it prepares the heart and spirit to receive. The preached word of God sets us up for a divine move. Usually when the average Christian hears the word of God preached some will develop a stopping point or a point of tolerance. Once an individual reaches his tolerance point, rejection begins to engage. The old traditional saying and I do quote, "It doesn't take all that". This becomes the foundation for rejection to take place. I have been in services where there was a great hunger and thirst for a move of God, but once the singing and preaching were over, there wasn't any room for the intense prophetic work to go forth. This is why in these cases one must prophesy while they are preaching or teaching. Many in the body of believers are not taught to receive anything after the singing and preaching have concluded, however one should not think it strange if God decides to release the prophetic after all the singing and preaching has gone forth. Those who seek God for greater moves are subject to appreciate God whether in an orthodox setting or from out behind the church walls.

When there is no singing, no praying, no preaching, and no praising, can the prophetic still operate? Of course it can. The prophetic anointing can appear even in a mere conversation. God's Spirit flows! It does not have to be worked up or pumped up as many think it has to. God's power flows freely to all that will allow it to. So we cannot put God in a box and say that there is only a certain way He is going to move. No matter how much we learn about God and the things of God, there is always some area of the unknown left for us to discover. There will always be new heights and new depths for us to enter in. Remember that it is the individual that puts the limit on God. It is the individual that put the stopping points and set the margins in his or her life when it comes to allowing God to move in our lives.

I would like to focus a while on the fulfilled and the unfulfilled. Many have experienced the prophet's ministry and many have witnessed the prophet giving a "word", maybe a word of promise, a word of warning, and word of direction or instruction. What causes a word to become fulfilled is when the word and time collaborate together. Yes, it is all about timing.

Jesus taught the parable about the sower of the seeds, explaining how the word fell on different types of ground. (Luke 8:12-15). The way side hearers are those that hear the word, then comes the devil and take away the word from their hearts that they may not believe and be saved. Then there are the hearers, that when they hear receive the word with too much emotion (joy) and these have no root. They believe for awhile but when trial and temptation came they fall away. Then there are the ones that fall among the thorns, which when they have heard the word, they go forth and are choked with the cares and riches and pleasures of life and bring no fruit to perfection. Finally there are the ones that fall on the good ground which represents having heard the word and they keep of the word and brings forth much fruit with patience.

Now let's consider the opposing factors that defeat the word and hinders it from lining up with time. In this parable the wayside hearer has a skeptical overview from the beginning. One might would think that God would not allow His word to be spoken to the skeptical, the untrusting and unbeliever. But God does and we submit these teachings to the skeptical by saying he that has an ear let him hear. The skeptical stands in a very critical position and don't believe many things that they hear. When the word lines up with time, we can experience the full benefit of God's promise. When we receive a word through the prophetic it is important for us to seek God on when would be the right time for us to respond or act on the word that was spoken over our lives. The rock hearer are the ones that are usually found in many high spirited church services. Rejoicing over the word so forcelly that they neglected to guard the word and allow it to penetrate to the depths of the heart, where it can be fully nourished to produce. Often times we can get overjoyed about good news and forsake to seek God's timing. The thorn hearer has allowed the word to penetrate enough to cause him or her to prosper but apparently in this parable the prosperity did not produce at the right time, as a result the riches and cares of this life choked the word and there was no maturity in the fruit. The bible encourages us that if we believe the prophet we will prosper (2 Chronicles 20:20). The good ground hearer believes the prophet, receives the word and keeps the word. What takes place when we keep the word? When we keep the word, we have applied it to our hearts and it has become part of our spiritual and mental makeup, and while we do this, we seek God for further instructions. That's when the word and time begin to line up properly to fulfill the word spoken over our lives. I can say that in my service as a minister, I have moved out of God's timing and it seemed like the word that was spoken over my life was not fulfilled. "We can do the right thing at the wrong time and it's just like doing the wrong thing at anytime." That was a quote from my first pastor and I never knew what it totally meant until I stepped out of God's timing. Many lives can be negatively effected when we don't operate in God's timing. Now my problem was I moved too fast, I was a rock hearer, as soon as I would hear the word I would start acting on it right away. It took some consequences and repercussion to discover that I had to let the word go deep enough to get protection and proper nourishment. So that I could experience the fulfillment of the word spoken over my life.

Many people have turned a deaf ear to the prophets and many have shunned the prophetic anointing. However, God is still using the prophets today and the prophetic anointing is still flowing through the community of Christian believers. It's easy to write a person off and call them a fake and a phony if a word of promise appears not to have materialized in our lives. I strongly urge the readers to check the word with the time. The word and time must work together respectfully in order to experience and receive the promises of God. In my personal experience and observations over the years, I have witnessed many victories in the lives of many people. Simply because they believed the prophet and allowed the word and time to work with God. I have also experienced victories simply by believing the prophet and allowing the word and time to work together.

When we experience the manifested promises of God it is like coming out of a battle with the victory. The time that elapse between the word of promise and the manifestation can vary, it is never the same but one thing you can always expect and that the opposer (the devil) will tempt us to do something or say something to hinder the promise from coming to pass. This is why when we get the manifested promise it is like a victory. In fact, it is a victory! It is God's desire for every believer to have the victory.

God gave us prophets to bring clarity to the believer and Christ to the sinner. God gave us prophets to bring direction to the bewildered, comfort to the troubled, warning to the rebellious, consequences to the disobedient, wealth to the poor, humbleness to the highminded. God gave us prophets to point out the areas in our lives that need our immediate attention, spiritual water to those that thirst and spiritual meat to those that hunger. The scripture states, "Blessed are they which do hunger and thirst after righteousness: for they shall be filled. (Matthew 5:6). There will be times when God uses the prophet to fill us. It is the words spoken by the prophet that fills us with peace, joy, hope, love, encouragement, Godly fear, trust, and faith.

The prophetic anointing enhances and empowers every gift in God's kingdom. The believer's authority also consists of the ability to speak to the various situations and obstacles that block their path and hinder their success. *The Lord says, "If ye had faith as a mustard seed, ye might say unto this sycamine tree, be thou plucked up by the root, and be thou planted in the sea; and it should obey you*". (Luke 17:6). So with our mouth we can decree and declare a thing over our life. Every believer should be encouraged to speak a victorious word over their life. We can have what we say. It is difficult for the believer sometimes but it is true and not impossible. Our words can form our destiny. *"Death and life are in the power of the tongue . . ."*(Proverbs 18:21). What seems to be the issue with some is that when the negative is spoken, it appears to happen more quickly then when the positive is spoken. The true believer should pattern themselves after the scriptures which tells us to" *be swift to hear and slow to speak . . ."* (James 1:19) in by doing, we will have direction on what to speak and when we should speak as we are directed by the Spirit of God. Then we will see and experience the power of God in operation.

As believers of God we should never give up on the things in which we have heard. Our faith in God and His promises should be enough to enable us to hold out until we are in the very presence of His promised word. Believers are sometimes prone to get weak and even fail in an area. The word says, *"And let us not be weary in well doing, for in due season we shall reap if we faint not."* (Galatians 6:9). We are to love God and keep His commandments, because

God is faithful. God is faithful to those who operate in his gifts and God is faithful to those who believe and benefit from those that operate in their anointings and gifts.

"Therefore we ought to give the more earnest heed to the things which we have heard, lest at any time we should let them slip."(Hebrews 2:1). Don't let the word slip away! Have an attentive ear so that the body of Christ can hear what the Spirit is saying in these last of the last days. To those who operate in the prophetic and for those who believe and benefit from the prophetic, that when frustration sets in because of an unmanifested promise. Remember it's only unmanifested because it appears unmanifested to us. God has a different time frame than humanity has. Even though we are made in His image and likeness, God is different from us. God has a set time to perform His word and it does not always line up with our timing. God's word will come to pass whether it was a spoken word or the written word. God's word will come to pass! Be encouraged to search the scriptures and notice the many ways God used His servants in the prophetic.

Are there Prophets today? Even though many may not believe that there are prophets today. The bible clearly states in Ephesians 4:11, "And He gave some Apostles, and some Prophets, and some Evangelists, and some Pastors and Teachers". God set these ministry gifts in the church and they are are as prevalent and effective today as they were in the days of old. It is the anointing that allows us to flow and operate with power. It is not of our own strengths and abilities, it is the power of God. So when the prophetic anointing is in operation, we should acknowledge God moving, believe that God is moving, receive what God is saying, receive what God is giving. When God is in the act of giving, it is so that the church, the body of Christ can be edified. Edification is what builds up the people of God. To be strong so that we may be able to operate in faith and love.

Let's not forget that it is every believers privilege to walk in power. Obedience is the key factor to walking in power. When we walk in obedience to God's word, it keeps the line clear. What line? The line of communication that's between the believer and God. When the line is clear there is no struggle in communicating with God. But when the believer constantly and wilfully disobey God, their communication to God is severly distorted and can lead to total blockage if the believer continues in diobedience. When a believer realizes that he or she has a divine gift, they should not take it lightly. Neither should they be deceived to think that they can walk in disobedience and God is still going to use them. God will not take away the gift from the believer but opportunties will cease for them to use their gifts. Nothing is worse than having a gift and no where to use it or anyone to share it with. So we as believers always want to stay in right standing with God.

We have covered the three P's that can motivate, stimulate, and activate the prophetic anointing. The three P's are prayer, praise, and preaching. If there is any doubt that an individual has a real prophetic anointing operating in their ministry, check to see if they are in submission to a leader. Yes, no matter how anointed or powerful we may be it is important that ministry gifts be in submission to another leader. The main reasons are accountability, development and discipline. One should never be found working in God's vineyard without proper supervision or accountability. This does not mean that there should always be someone looking over our shoulders when we are ministering, but we as labours must realize that we are all members fitly joined together. That each gift and each office compliments the other. If an individual chooses to operate alone or without a covering they can set themselves up for failure and unnecessary blame.

It is difficult to submit to leadership if that leadership does not operate, understand or believe in the gifts that are operating in ones life. The bible says that the spirit of the prophet is subject to the prophet (1 Corintians 14:32). Which also let's us know that the prophet should be submitted to another prophet in order to be in line with God's order of doing things. The 21st century church is in it's infancy stage and a lot of ideas on how we should conduct ourselves and carry out God's order are rapidly changing, however, somethings won't ever change. One of them is submission to leadership. If a prophet is subject to a pastor or Bishop, the prophet must learn how to flow or operate in the prophetic according to the order of the local church that they are a part of. The bible states that our gift will make room for us and bring us before mighty men. (Proverbs 18:16). So even if the opportunity doesn't arise in the local church, God will make provision for the prophet to operate in his or her gift. If the prophet is subject to a Pastor or Bishop that is also prophetic, they have a greater benefit to have their gift developed. When gifts are the same not only do they compliment each other but they also strengthen each other. Just like iron sharpening iron.

Discipline is a very important necessity to the prophetic anointing. As I forestated everything that God reveals to the prophet, does not necessarily have to be spoken out. Discipline helps the prophet or the one flowing in the prophetic anointing, speak in God's timing. Sometimes things that God reveal is for an individuals own personal benefit such as warning of danger or life threatening situations. If a person is operating under the influence of the prophetic anointing and have no discipline, it is very possible that he or she may cause more harm than good. Simply because of the lack of submission to leadership. Some might would argue this point by saying that the Holy Spirit disciplines their prophetic anointing and that can be well and true but let's be realistic. Every believer has or should have a natural and spiritual leader. We are not always in the realm of spirituality because we are confined in a terrestrial (earthly) body which is subject to terrestrial (earthly) conditions and because of that we won't always hearken to the Holy Spirit. That's when our natural, tangible leader that is inspired and consecrated by God can step in and instruct, encourage, inspire and direct us if necessary. That is when discipline is developed because of the sensitivity connected to the prophetic anointing. Discipline is very important. Discipline helps maintain balance in behavior, appearance and reputation in the 21st century church.

The way we conduct ourselves, the way we present ourselves (image), and our reputation (service record) plays a vital part in the way we are received when standing before a congregation. Let's consider John the Baptist as He walked in the prophetic anointing. The Apostle John as the bible states in John 1:8 was sent to bear witness of the Light. The Light was indeed Jesus Christ. In bearing witness many thought that John the Baptist was a prophet. John denied being a prophet though he was used prophetically. In the gospels of Mark, Luke,and John you may notice that each of these gospel portray the conduct, image and the reputation of his ministry. Under the prophetic anointing John's conduct was unorthodoxed to the Jewish customs however because he quoted the Prophet Isaiah, some were able to understand. Mark 1:6 talks about John's image by stating what he wore and what he ate which was apparently outstanding from the customs of the people that he was ministering to. All three Gospels, Mark, Luke and John records the reputation and service record of John the Baptist. They included him as being a forerunner and foreteller of Jesus' coming. In by doing so, this would cause the hearers to perceive him as a prophet. John introduced the baptism of repentance in Luke 3:3. This was the doctrine never before heard by man. These were the basic yet monumental records of John the Baptist's mission. This shows us that the prophetic anointing in a person's life can cause them to stand out and when the person stands out he or she may feel or appear different or strange. That is where the discipline comes in. Discipline comes in and causes the emotions to come in subjection to the Holy Spirit so that one can flow with the spirit with ease and maintain true confidence in God and in ones self since the prophetic anointing makes an individual spontaneous. It is sometimes difficult to harness these abilities into subjection. Those who flow in the prophetic anointing may find it difficult from time to time to do the same thing in the same way for a long period of a time. Actually prophetic people often don't think of themselves as strong, but when guided by proper discipline, feelings of inadequacy, doubt or even fear can easily be resolved.

The 21st century church is still in battle and have not fully embraced the prophetic however we are seeing more and more of the prophetic anointing being ushered into the traditional congregation that have never believed in such a move of God. When prophecy is manifested or has come to pass, it strengthens the unbelieving and wavering faith and it is converted into believing, non-doubting faith. When a believer can accept a spoken word (RHEMA) under the prophetic anointing, he or she will witness that this word will bring confirmation, clarity, direction, comfort, and even warning. It is given to the believer to make improvements in thier life.

The 21st century church is now and will in the future see more ministers operate under the prophetic anointing. People are in need of a word fresh from heaven's vault. Preachers and teachers are now and in the future will be found flowing in and operating under the prophetic anointing. Be mindful that a minister that is ministering under the prophetic anointing is not always Foretelling or giving a prediction about the future. There are other areas involved and what we are witnessing today are words given that fits a certain situation. In other words, it is a preached or taught word that suits an immediate need whereas in some instances we could not receive what we need to hear in the traditional homeletical sermon.

In this age of informaton and high technology an individual can obtain a sermon from several sources on any given day. A sermon can be bought in books, CD or DVD, pulled up online, texted over the cell phone, however, a divinely appointed word spoken under the prophetic anointing can not be obtained from these methods. A sermon is planned and prophetic word is unplanned, a sermon can be rehearsed, a prophetic word is unrehearsed, a sermon is a collection of information and thoughts formally written and outlined. A prophetic word is given through the utterance of the Holy Spirit in a known or unknown language. A sermon doesn't always give confirmation. A prophetic word always give confirmation. A sermon is read, a word is spoken. A sermon is delivered, a prophetic word will cause the hearer to be delivered. Now we have given a few contrast between a sermon and a word, keep in mind that a prophetic word is believed to be divinely inspired. It is a term used in the 21st century church that describes a spontaneous utterance that correlate with the hearers immediate needs. The sermon is prepared and even though the sermon is prepared with prayer and meditation it could take several days to prepare. Even though the sermon is excepted as the proper way to address a congregation or the general public, there is an elected group of ministers that may remain faithful to their topic or subject of their sermon but not faithful to the manuscript. Some call it 'when the

Holy Spirit pulls you off the paper'. The written sermon usually serves as a foundation as the prophetic speaker waits on the prophetic anointing to manifest. This technique of ministering the word is widely spreading across every denominational line and is practiced in preaching, teaching and evangelizing.

So as John the Baptist, all the major and minor prophets of the bible, many kings of the bible and even Jesus spoke words that God told them to speak without any formal manuscript. So we should not think it so strange if the word is being delivered without a manuscript. Let the prophetic anointing flow as you minister. Hearers of the word shouldn't try to discredit a minister that doesn't speak from a manuscript, God uses everybody different. The gifts of God comes from God, they are not bought in a store neither can they be obtained from a classroom. But the more a person learn about a particular thing, the better they can relate to and understand, as a result one can enjoy the benfits. If an individual does not possess a certain gift of God, the more the individual should pray and learn about the gift the better they can relate to and understand it. As a result they will be able to enjoy the benefits of that gift simply by receiving the benefits without fear, doubt and unbelief.

The best way to learn about the prophetic is to be in enviroments where the prophetic anointing is in operation. Not necessarily a particular denomination, but connected with people that believe that there are still prophets today and that they flow and know how to flow in the prophetic. Even though the prophetic anointing cannot be obtained in a classroom, there are various books to help you understand the prophetic anointing. The study of scriptures, run cross references, the study of historical prophets are also ways to understand and learn of the prophetic anointing. One must truly believe God not only moved in ancient times but that He moves today in the 21st century. Remember, Jesus Christ the same yesterday, and today and forever.(Hebrews 13:8).

God made man in His image and likeness. As a result we are created free moral agents, that gives us the right to choose, the power of choice. Unbelief is a result of a choice and unbelief is such a powerful force. It is powerful enough to hinder God's manifestations. Unbelief destroys our faith and unbelief will cause one not to experience a move of God. When bound by unbelief it causes you to tie God's hand. Fear is a learned behavior and our fears usually comes from someone that has great influence on your life, whatever they fear, you will fear it too. People that fear God in a negative way are influenced by people who fear Him in a negative way.

Every good and perfect gift comes from above . . . (James 1:17). Every gift that God has sent is sent to build up His people. Understanding is the best mental power that will conquer fear. The bible says, "In all thy getting, get understanding." (Proverbs 4:17). Love is the only emotion tht conquers fear, 1 John 4:18a says, "There is no fear in love; but perfect love casteth out fear". Doubt causes a person to become double-minded. In other words there will be a part of a person that says "I believe" and the other part will say, "but it's not going to happen for me" with these two thoughts combating against each other, one can develop a double mind and a double-minded man is unstable in all his ways. (James 1:8). In order to overcome doubt and be at peace, one must keep his or her mind stayed on the Lord. "Thou will keep him in perfect peace whose mind is stayed on Thee."(Isaiah 26:3). The hour has come that the prophet is coming to the front line. And those that have an ear to hear, should be willing to hear what the Spirit is saying to the church, to the nations and to the world.

I previously mentioned that the fivefold ministry gifts symbolized the hand of God, the Apostles, the Prophets, the Evangelists, the Pastors and Teachers. Each one of these ministry gifts or offices represents a finger on the mighty hand of God. The prophetic anointing can operate freely in any of these ministry gifts. Just as the prophetic is controversial so is the ministry of the Apostle. Many religious sects teach that the Apostles no longer exist. The Webster-Collegiate Dictinary defines the Apostle as a special messenger sent by God. The Scriptures notes that one of the main duties of the Apostle was to establish and set churches in order. The prophetic anointing equips the Apostle today as he or she operates in that particular gift. The Apostle does not usually pattern themselves after any of their peers or fellowlabours. They are original in nature, they burn their on trials and when an Apostle speaks under the influence of the prophetic anointing, there is usually a positioning of God's people in the local, district, state, national or worldwide level of the church, so that God's will can be carried out efficiently. When the Apostle speaks under the influence of the prophetic anointing the exhorting of God's people will be in effect. To exhort means to warn and the warning also sets God's house in order.

The Prophet as defined previously as a messenger, one that foretells and forthtells and has the ability to operate spontaneously. The Prophet is the one that will be more close in tune with the prophetic anointing because the Prophet is governed by and inspired by the prophetic anointing. When the Prophet speaks, he or she will always be speaking under the influence of the prophetic anointing, but their vocal abilities will not be always the same. It will be according to the circumstances, atmosphere or setting they are in. As Isaiah was commanded to lift his voice like a trumpet (Isaiah 58:1), this is symbolic for a calling of attention. This is one of the primary duties of the prophet to call God's people attention to their transgressions. There may be instances when God's people get distracted and take a wrong direction in life that same "trumpet", the voice of the Prophet can get God's people back on the right track. Because the voice of the Prophet has pointed out the error of His people. The Prophet is used to exhalt and edify, which means to build up, encourage, and give hope to.

The Evangelist has a broader territory to cover and is not effective in the local church as he or she would be in the "field". The scripture explains it as going into all the world. "And He said unto them, Go ye into all the world and preach the gospel to every creature". (Mark 16:15). The Evangelist ultimate goal is to spread God's word to as many outside of the church as possible. When the Evangelist speaks under the influence of the prophetic anointing it always concludes with an invitation to except Christ as their personal Lord and Saviour. This is why the word of God instructs us to do the work of an evangelist. (2 Timothy 4:5). There are things that the Evangelist will speak that a stationary minister like the Pastor or Teacher wouldn't speak, because the Evangelist would not have to return back to the congregation as a nurturer, instructor or counselor. In laymen terms, the Evangelist has the liberty to speak whatever they have to speak and move on to the next mission. The prophetic anointing helps the Evangelist adjust to different and new environments since the evangelistic ministry requires travel and moving around.

The Prophetic anointing benefits the Pastor in preaching, teaching and even in the development of the vision for the church. Since the Pastor is a more stationary position in the church, the Pastor with the gift of prophecy should strongly seek God about how to flow in that gift without bringing confusion into the church. Everyone in the church do not understand this kind of anointing. It is wise that the Pastor flow in the prophetic in other areas than personal prophecies. There are times when God sends a prophecy to the local church as a whole and this should be done by the set man or woman of the house. But if prophecy is given by someone other than the Pastor, then the Pastor should be able to confirm the prophecy for that congregation, because the Pastor is the undershepherd of that flock. The prophetic anointing can assist the Pastor when he or she has a very tight schedule and time does not permit them to prepare a homeletical sermon outline or manuscript. As we reflect back we conclude that the prophetic has a spontaneous quality and this can allow the Pastor to be spontaneous in his preaching and teaching the word of God. However, Pastors or any other minister that flows in the prophetic should not let this anointing hinder them from studying and searching the scriptures. Pastors should remember that they have to stay around and return to their congregation wherein some of the ministry gifts such as the Evangelist does not necessarily have to return to a local congregation as a pastor. A Pastor should never want to hear one of his parishioners question them with these words, "Pastor, I thought you said". Church members will also use words like, "Pastor remember when you said" or "what did you mean when you said?" So as a Pastor whatever is spoken will come back to you and hopefully not to bite you!

The Teacher and their relationship to the prophetic anointing is similar as the Pastor because much preparation of information has to take place in order to teach in the 21st century church. People like work books, work sheets, and they like to take notes. This is the information era and people today are big on information. "Give me the facts" is one of the noted statements of the century. The teacher has a lot of explaining to do, therefore, the prophetic anointing is most effective with the teacher when questions are asked that does not relate to a prepared lesson. The prophetic anointing will also assist the teacher in preparing their lesson by revealing certain situations that needs to be dealt with. When a Teacher speaks under the prophetic anointing the results should produce clarity and understanding.

The hearer of the word of God whether it be the written word or the spoken word, may want to bring into question some of the things in which they have heard. The hearer's main concern should be focused on the prophetic word spoken directly to them. If an individual is confronted by someone speaking under the prophetic anointing, there are a few things the individual should consider.

First, is the word spoken to them confirmation of a particular event, plan, situation, or circumstance in their life that they are already aware of. Second, are the words being spoken bringing attention to the speaker or bringing glory to God. Thirdly, are the words being spoken bring clarity and understanding to something that's occurring already in your life. Next, are the words being spoken point out or bring a certain thing to your attention and give warning. And finally, are the words being spoken pointing you in a direction that you should take and help you make the best and the right decision. If the answer is yes to any of these considered points and the words spoken brings attention and glory to God then you know you are getting a true word from God from a true vessel of God. Yes, God speaks clearly and effectively through His people today and in the 21st century church. We can expect to see more of the prophetic in operatin in these closing hours of time. Be encouraged to embrace this anointing when it is manifested. Be watchful and prayerful, for we should also know that everything God has Satan has a counterfeit copy. But if these basic truths are applied, you will be able to identify what is taking place in your presence.

Many people today are enjoying the benefits and blessings, healings and miracles, joy and strength, peace and hope, simply because of a word spoken to them under the prophetic anointing. If you can believe you to can receive.

"Jesus said unto him, If thou canst believe, all things are possible to him that believeth. (Mark 9:23). Faith cometh by hearing and hearing by the word of God. (Romans 10:17). The more that person hears the word of God, the stronger their faith becomes. It is our faith that causes things of God to operate in our lives. It is impossible to benefit from the prophetic anointing without faith. It is faith that carries us beyond what we can comprehend.

The movement of God can only be explained to a certain degree. When things begin to happen that we cannot explain totally, then we can earnestly say that our faith is in full effect. God has a unique way of overwhelming mankind. Even men and women of great depth, knowledge and wisdom have experienced an unexplainable event in their lives when they could only say that it was God moving in their behalf. Those of great intellect are sometimes to proud to admit their divine encounters, but inwardly they know that the unexplainable experience was God in action. God has used so many people in so many ways in the prophetic and it only lets us know that there is really no set way, that God choses to use mankind.

There are some who were so profound in the prophetic that they were commanded to remove their shoes permanently as a sign to the doubtful and unbelieving. They had to endure severe heat and cold weather conditions, some even worked in dangerous environments. But the taking off of the shoes was an act of reverence and obedience to God. It is also a sign that the prophet is walking in that anointing continuously. Many servants of God operate in an anointing until it passes and then there are others that walk in the prophetic anointing continuously. There are some that remove their shoes only when they are ministering in the prophetic in a church service or some other formal service like a revival or crusade. Then there are some others who never remove their shoes. It is safe to say that the intensity of the prophetic anointing cannot be determined by how one takes his or her shoes off. This goes to show us just how versatile God is. Keep in mind that the outward things that we portray is to bring glory to God and not ourselves.

Timing is very important if any one receives a word under the prophetic anointing. The spoken word and God's time has to properly line up together. We should not always pass judgment when we don't instantly see the results of a word spoken under the prophetic anointing manifest in your life. The 21st century church has experienced a long season of shifting and change in structure. It is going to take a strong hand of God to govern and guide the 21st century church to her destiny. Just like in the days of old. God used kings to govern His people but when God really wanted to speak, He had to use the Prophets. When the Prophets season had elapsed God had to send His Son. Look at the order, Prophets before the Son. Jesus is soon to return and the Prophetic is making it's final call in the earth. In the day you hear His voice, harden not your hearts. This is the season, this is the Prophetic before the second coming of the Lord, Jesus Christ. The fact remains the same as written in the book of 2 Chronicle 20:20, ". . . . believe His prophets so shall ye prosper". Don't think it strange when you begin to see preachers and teachers step away from their manuscript and speak profoundly on God's behalf. Think it not strange when someone points you out or call you forth and speak words of confirmation, instruction or exaltation over the situation in your life. Think it not strange when your typical traditional church service transforms into a radical spiritual awakening as in the day of Pentecost. Think it not strange when a word is brought forth in the supermarket or at the barbershop, maybe even at the flea market. A word that change your entire perception of life or even saved the unsaved. It is merely the Prophetic Anointing in operation as spoken to us by the Prophet Joel, "And it shall come to pass afterward, that I will pour out my spirit upon all flesh; and your sons and your daughters shall prophesy . . . (Joel 2:28a). Be blessed and enjoy the gifts that God has given to us.

Made in the USA
Columbia, SC
10 February 2022